Poetry Nook

Volume 1
September 2013

Frank Watson, Editor
Tiara Winter-Schorr, Associate Editor

Plum White
Press

Published by Plum White Press LLC

For information concerning reprints, email:
followingtheblueflute@gmail.com

ISBN-13: 978-1-939832030
ISBN-10: 1939832039
LCCN: 2013917427
BISAC: Poetry / Anthologies

Cover design copyright © 2013 by Frank Watson

Cover image, "Surrealistic Head," copyright Slava Gerj, licensed
via Shutterstock.com, 2013

Published in the United States of America

Table of Contents

.

$100 PRIZES

FOR POETRY AND ART

We will announce the winners of the poetry and art prizes in next month's issue. Both art and photography will be eligible for the art prize. Reader feedback will be an important element in awarding the prizes, so please send your feedback on the poetry and art you like to Frank Watson at followingtheblueflute@gmail.com.

Love Must You Stealthily Come

Love must you stealthily come to me
When I am least prepared for you
Not to mention I haven't even read
The morning newspaper

Ryan Derham

I Must be In Love

I must be in love.
Now I'm about to go out
and hunt out the drop
of water in the river
that I caught a glitter of.

Akiko Taylor

Some Words

Some words
bite
on the way
out.

Chris Smith

Seduced Into the Desert

I will seduce my love, lead her into the desert, and speak to her heart. ~
Hosea 2:16

Seduced and led as surely as if shackled and noosed,
I've wound up in the desert. But don't get me wrong—
this is no wailing song. Far from it this call for
celebration acknowledging the soul's penetration
by earth's beauty, creation's oneness—caught up
in the rhythm and flow of desert seasons,

sparseness, apparent emptiness opening wide the heart
to scarcity, hunger, thirst. No place for the fainthearted as inborn,
biophilic needs awaken; and I—
shaken out of complacency—seek out the secretive ones,
following footprints, body indentations across the sand,
sometimes yearning for those days trolling marsh edges

with Snowy egrets, marveling how Great Blue herons stand
frozen for hours stabbing sunfish and gar, how White ibis
grub in the mud for crawfish while Reddish egrets cast wing
shadows over their prey and those ingenious Green herons
drop fish bits as bait into the slough—their patience to wait
forever enviable. And I would trade a thousand nights

sleeping on silk sheets, all my treasured books—
everything but my passion for life to live among
those sensual shapely beauties, to be swaddled
in the gauzy purple mists sunrise sunset as I synthesize
with them all the elements of the grassy river.
But back to the present, the desert, which is as well a gift—

less flamboyant than the Everglades, but once I let the sidra
tree speak to me, I was a goner—the dunes singing,
shamal wind winding around the rim of the Inland Sea.
So here, too, I watch and wait for a chance to participate
in synthesis—a guest trying my very best not to be
invasive in this far from empty desert.

Diana Woodcock

Monsoon Lessons

After silence of drought, such speech.
From ephemeral alphabets traced in the mud
I'm learning the grammar of rain,
linguistics of flood.

But puddles are illegible
or too murky for strangers to read:
some message about pain
in the wet stammer of weed.

The sun declares the lesson over.
Hardly mastered. In dried ground
spelling crumbles. There remain
only punctuating buds around

what had been sentences. Next storm
I may learn to decipher earth's half
of cloud's thought, or fail again
to finish one fertile paragraph.

Elisavietta Ritchie

I Am the Purpose for Your Flaws

I am the purpose for your flaws
Your darkness & beauty
For they fit so perfectly with mine

L.B. Austin

Feast

Skin tattooed with flame
conceals an icy sweetness.
Apples for breakfast.

Marion Adams

School Custard

Tom Swanston

And If We Go Down

And if we go down
let it be a
soft
sweet
destruction.

Chris Smith

Dahlia After a Rainstorm

I pour grape juice for Stan who's
always in a hurry. 7:50 A.M. Rain

does all sorts of naughty things on the roof.
I shudder to think what the neighbors will say,

but we don't discuss the weather—
only ponderous subjects. Hello

leads to Heidegger. Who? Raindrops
sharpen like my sixth-grade teachers tongue.

I want to fight back but stay indoors:
dry air, a coat made of nudity. When

it lets up, I walk in the garden, want to see
if my friends are alright—no,

the Tom Edison dahlia cut in half,
a fat purple blossom on the ground.

I hold the broken half in my casket arms,
when the sun comes out at noon

to lead a funeral. Each pallbearer wears
a purple suit jacket.

A sudden breeze
carries the soul into autumn's chilly halls.

Kenneth Pobo

The Green of Absinthe

the green of absinthe
is the colour of magic
chasing the fairy...

LazyBookWorm

Redneck Girl

redneck girl—
her first car
was a pickup truck

M. Kei

His First Job

his first job,
paid in pizza and
cash under the table

M. Kei

The Last Love of Icarus

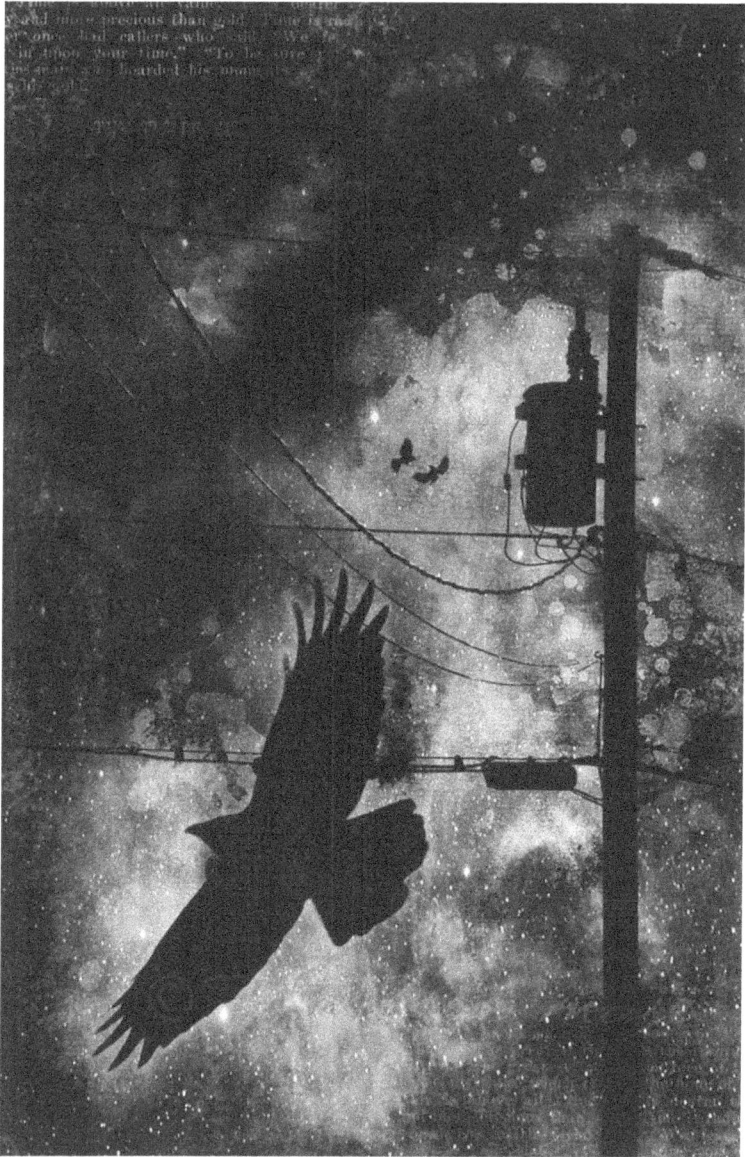

Kelly Letky

The Last Love of Icarus

all day long i listen to the song
of grasshoppers, crickets, and beetles

    after a time, i can hear nothing else

the buzz of a hummingbird sipping nectar
from windowbox purple petunias
shifts me from there to here

    again

        and again

        and i marvel at wings
        quite literally
        spun from sugar

you drive into the world of concrete jungle

    you drive into the world

you drive

    away

    as i walk these paths
    choked with weeds and chewed up leaves

pulling a cloak of clouds over your shoulder
to remind me that the stars are always lit

    and i am here

here

    with only these crows for company

some days they tell me of your travels

some days they carry me to grace

some days they peck at my shiny rings
as i reach for the sky with lost fingers

some days
they bring me
white feathers

held in beaks flecked with blood, stardust

and gold

Kelly Letky

Come Sway with Me

Come sway with me
Catch the moon by the tip of his tongue
Let's make him blush
A bright, icy pink

Rhonda Brockmeyer

Cold at Night

cold at night
in this brown house
without you
or your tempered moans
between my lips.

Matsukaze

In This Garden

I stir from the motionless depths,
coming close to the new face
that wants to be my own.
Harsh like light to the sleeping eye,
my roots are torn and my seed
is yet of the earth.
I reach back and then beyond —
all my poems are with me now,
it is the accumulation of my soul's dance,
it is the rejoicing and the coldness of loss.
Around, around - so close to the daylight,
shaking without the shade.
If I had lived before, then now I am thrown
behind the door where eternity, not life abides.
Mortal year that has replaced my air
with this huffing and bewilderment -
how strong was the wave that has washed me over.
There are great things to come, though Death
has forever changed the shape of my smile

Allison Grayhurst

The 19ᵗʰ Century

Ruined gardens
Acres of rampant phlox
And rhododendron jungles

Grape arbored walk
Caving on hoops
Black moss
Creeping over broken paving stones

Corinthian columns
Of old reflecting pools
Fallen in the grass
Like Roman numerals

Winged lion chair
Crumbling in sun
Where a foundation gapes
Like a vast mouth
Filling with scum-water

Japanese gardens
Throttling in the grip
Of oak roots enormous
As sumo wrestlers

Wooden bridge
Humping a pond choked
With algae
Antique goldfish flashing
Like coins down a sewer

Teahouse locked
Tatami mats unrolled
Ceremonies that no longer exist

In 19th century photographs
Everything shone
Gilt as money
An estuary like this
Offering privacy
From river traffic

Espaliered trees
Hedges clipped like elephants
And leopards
Women with parasols
And pale unsmiling faces
Posed by iron gates
Dislocating year by year
Like wishes

A stone eagle
Mourning the loss of its right wing
Illegible inscriptions

On a promontory
An abandoned lighthouse
Conjures how the river
Throbbed with barges

Joan Colby

The Heart's Geography

the heart's geography,
an unmapped place
with no landmarks

M. Kei

JD Blues

It's a Jack Daniels
1970's BG's high.
It's a heart that hurts
hangs on, hung over heavy,
bar hops, bee bop
booze and blues
satin and silk
sorry nights.

Norma Ketzis Bernstock

Tourism

No other spire
can be this spire.

We see it rise just
out of the mist,

a ship
or photograph

arriving,
developing.

How can we know
we are truly

here or merely
imagining in advance?

Air, or blood?

Let us sip another
coffee, dip a second cake

and try
to inscribe this

in our bones—a crypt
of memories

we visit
like saints

whose feet
we sometimes kiss.

David Radavich

She Wears

she wears
black bondage pants with
a Winnie the Pooh t-shirt
how awkward
to be thirteen!

M. Kei

Monsters

when i sleep
the monsters of my imagination
go away
and the real monsters
come out
to play

Michael Seese

And So

and so,
the grief of
childhood
and the bruises
on his knuckles

M. Kei

For Basquiat (1960-88)

You murder syntax, squeeze language,
upend pencil, charcoal, paint,
anything that makes a mark.

Your rage tops Picasso's --
you scream on canvas --
birding, jiving, repeating shit --
everyone is watching.

Torn between black and white,
black and blue, flaming with Andy --
body reeling for a fix,
you both are dying
faster than you're
being eaten by sharks.

With eyeblasting hallucinations,
baring your bones, you gallop
Death down the last laugh.

Jan Garden Castro

Children of the World

Photography by

Alec Goldwyn & Grace Brignolle

The following pages are a collection of photographs from three different countries. The children shown here are of various socioeconomic backgrounds, races, and cultures. Our aim is to not only show the differences among them but to highlight the commonalities. The images depict their gaze, their moods, their light, and the ever-present innocence that pervades their being, regardless of their living conditions.

Tiara Winter-Schorr

Alec Goldwyn

Alec Goldwyn

Alec Goldwyn

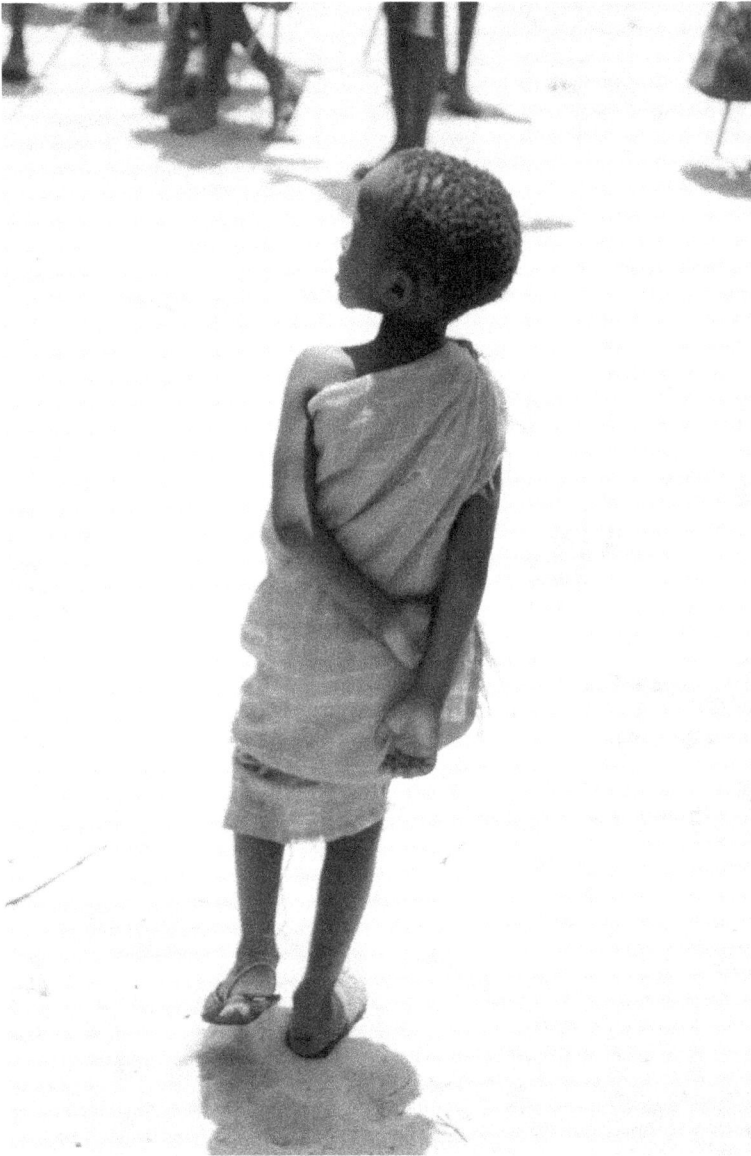

Alec Goldwyn

Alec Goldwyn

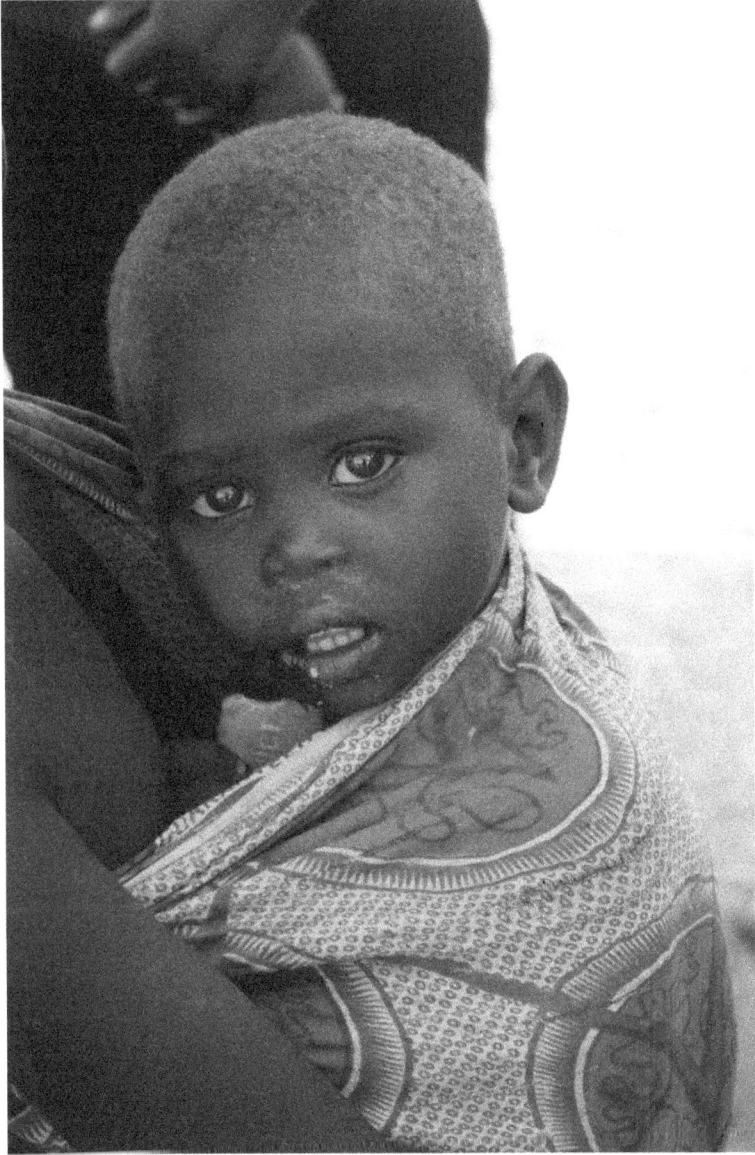

Alec Goldwyn

Alec Goldwyn

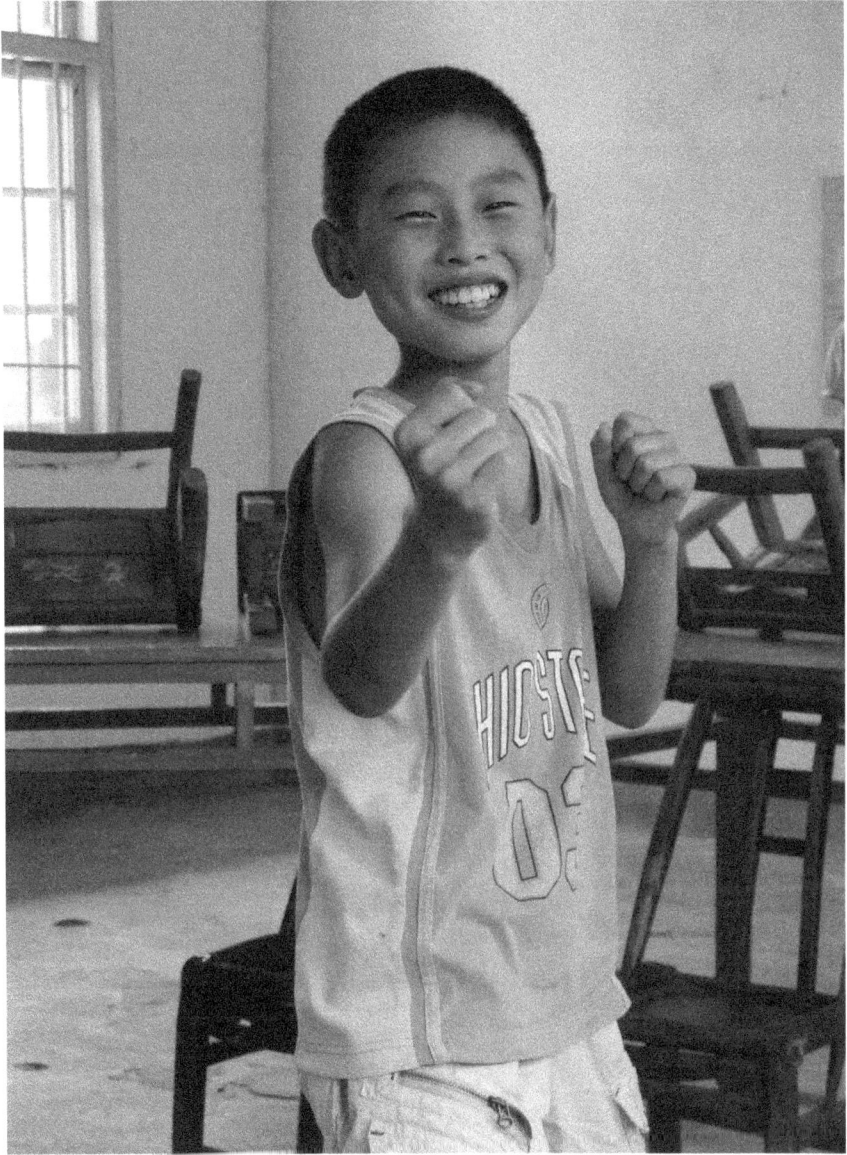

Alec Goldwyn

Grace Brignolle

Grace Brignolle

Houses

One house burns,
a lamp falls, cracks,
the flames climb
the walls, cross
the beams.
A great crane—
its wings upswept,
head pointing
towards the sky—
burns. The delicate
feathers blacken.
The flames don't
seem to touch it.
Yet it shrinks.
It cracks and falls.

Standing by the road,
the children watch
the orange flicker.
What does it
matter if one
house burns?
We will always
find another.

Daryl Muranaka

Dante and We

stumble on hot stones
brimming with lava,
tiptoe over ash
reeling,
rewind ourselves to
awaken
in the middle
of a dark forest
stunned
by murky remembrances,
ready
to chop wood.

Mary Harwell Sayler

Selkie's Way

Fish make good company,
but I want to touch a man's body,
touch his conversation,

even his soul. I shed
my seal skin and look for him.
Perhaps I have 2 souls,

part seal, part human.
On land, I dream of the sea's
dark depths. In water,

I dream of poplars and kettles.
Love must be where water
rushes up to a dry beach,

the point of intersection.
I crave that point,
take joy when all seems lost,

when my man walks back
to his home and I slip
under the waves.

Kenneth Pobo

Cape Province, South Africa, 1940s

I must be two and a half
or maybe three years old
we've just returned from the beach
we're climbing the stairs to our guesthouse
I feel terribly hot,
the sun was blazing this afternoon
you're just behind me,
then suddenly I see you fall
and slip down the stairs, like a ragged doll,
but with a heavy thump,
the vision is frightening.
Mamica, Mamica, I want to scream,
but nothing comes out of my mouth
and I stare blankly, minutes pass like hours,
someone has heard the noise
then I see two pairs of naked legs
approaching us
they're long, muscled and very tanned,
two men in kaki shorts lift Mamica
and bring her to our room.
I follow, sobbing; the landlady reassures me,
«your mommy will be all right,
we have called the doctor, don't worry, dear.»
That is the first time
I witness your suffering, Mamica,
and what a shock it is to see you,
my pillar of strength, my lovely-looking mother
unconscious, or dead? I'm not sure
- what does dead mean, anyway -
at the mercy of strangers
and me, me, your adoring son,
powerless, all alone, stiff like a statue,
but with a heart that hurts so much,
I still cannot utter a word.
«Just a sunstroke!» says the doctor,
«give her this,» he tells our landlady,
«she'll recover soon, but
don't let her go back
to the sea before a few days.»

Albert Russo

43

Reflection in the Stars

a child
sips noiselessly from the stars
as the moon returns to oblivion

upon the sidewalk
she sees her shadow
and recognizes herself

looking down from the mountaintop
the clouds remember song
as a child leaps with joy

John Reinhart

Aware

I am sitting on the edge
of the River.
The River is so wide—
it is coursing, foaming, overwhelming
in its bounty. I scarcely
need to reach in—and out springs
everything imaginable: Art,
soul, happiness, purpose.

No, not sitting on, I *am* the edge,
the shore, the bed soaked
in the River's bliss.
And all this water is me too!
Wet, watery, softer than earth,
sheer magic movement.
I move among the selves of this world
and I am.

Janine Canan

Historic Home

The draperies pool on the floor
Folds of crushed velvet
"to prevent drafts," the guide says, but practicality
is second thought. The reason is style. Victorian
visages cantilever
over our heads. They never smile
in early photographs. Posing as classic
authorities, they dignify
themselves with a nod to reason.

The chairs are stiff and formal. Interiors
The shade of old wine. A funeral wreath of hair
Over the mantel. Carpets fading with design.

We pass through this
Restoration. How they lived
Seems comfortless, remote. The fashionable child
In the oval frame is pale, Enormous eyes,
 enveloped in ruffles of white.
Pensive as if the blight
Of time edged his thought.

Joan Colby

Leaf Collage

Daniela Gioseffi

Sorescu's Core

in honor of a Romanian poet

Marin, I've been staring
at the painting that you did
as a cover for translations
of your poems: a bowl
of fruit, well-suited to design
the colorful plump phrases
pared to sink your teeth
into the pulp of apples,
oranges, lemons, life-sliced
and spiced and eaten with
your hands
behind your back, elbows
akimbo, juice
dripping
            down my chin.

Mary Harwell Sayler

Come Send Me

Come send me
To beautiful damnation
And leave there no doubt how far I will fall

L.B. Austin

As Above, So Below

Your heat transfers to the surface of my brain
when you touch down on the planet we own and
set your sweat-hot boots aside to rest on me. In me,
like I am the rock that formed around your molten core.
I'm not afraid. You have the same ice eyes you had
as a boy and those lashes, like thirty lashes, still flick me
with their secret code. *Don't look now. I dare you to laugh.*
Did you ever sit out on the porch and watch a hot prairie
storm form over the fields, laying down the corn like a lover,
while I sat watching two miles away as the lightning pointed
out your family land and lit up the wind overhead?
Of course you have. Well, that.
My heart is the same hot storm even now.

Angelique Cain

I'm Too Close

I'm too close
touch me
I will
burn.

Chris Smith

A Series of Tanka

we lay in heavy dew
on the city boulevard
sky eyes open
sifting aurora's seven veils
through our fingers

           in the Valley of Ten Peaks
           we walked on clouds
           gathering bouquets of wild rain
           the first time you said
           you loved me

how the mountain's breath
caught and held us
in a shower of meteors
beneath earth's blue umbrella
we splashed in puddles of light

           on the night
           lightning pinned
           my splayed wings
           to the charred breast of earth
           I became a quivering dragonfly

in the loft
among sweet bales of hay
we sleep
with deer mice nibbling
the chaff of our city dreams

we are cloud-smudged
on a graphite sky
blending and erasing
the sketched lines of our belonging
until this paper life is thin

breathe into me
the fossil memory of moss
breathe into me
the dust of ancient meditations
I arise, a bird

in kettled-tidepool
purple sea stars cling
to ungranted wishes
we scatter the dust of ourselves
into the drowning sea

I unfold my origami self
and swim into a lake of fire
washing my hair in ashes
the crane-legged words
of a thousand burning poems

Debbie Strange

Trapped Inside

trapped inside
my dilemma
a luna moth dreams
of taking flight
on the wrong side of the glass window.

elle M.

I Painted My Dreams

I painted my dreams on slides of glass
And folded them carefully,
In Eastern silk.
I walked West until I walked into the sea.

Graeme Cooper

Insomnia Cantatas

For A. L., who complains that when he has not written for several days, he feels ill.

These interruptions, I have known:
midnight gunfire, burglars, hurricane,
a lover or the lack, tidal flood,

that sudden rush of blood
and, more frequent now, the pierce of pain—
my malformed bones.

This is just another broken night,
of late more rare
thanks to makeshift peace, and age and locks,

though one nocturnal thief, a rusty fox,
steals indoors to filch the kitten's fare.
Simply: I did not write

all day—
no, many days when barren pages
heap like futile clouds or arctic snows,

and wasted brilliance flows—
snowflakes melting into rain—and I must hide my rage
as unused hours swirl down the drain, away

and gone—
Such nights I wake at four
or barely sleep at all.

Thank God *this* winter night I hear the calls
of tundra swans camped in the cove, unlock the door
to let in swan cantatas, hungry fox, lover, words, and not too soon, the
    dawn.

Elisavietta Ritchie

56

Cicada

cicada
this summer night
calling me home—
i go where there
is song

Sondra J. Byrnes

Alligator Boots

The Ku Klux Klan used to
thunder down Main Street
in my hometown
on horses,
with their white sheets
and hoods, like a
mountain of marching snowmen,
in 4th of July parades
up until the 1950s.
I remember one year
my grandfather, not normally
a drinker, was lit up
on some beers,
and ran up to one of
the men on the horses
and called out
the name Harry.
And the man leaned down
in acknowledgment.
I heard my grandfather yell,
"I knew it was you, from those
shit kickin' alligator boots of yours."
They were both laughing
as my grandfather, jumping up a little,
pulled Harry's hood
from his head.
My grandfather ran
back to my dad
and me on the sidewalk,
laughing with hood in hand.
Harry continued down the street
on his horse, seemingly unaffected
by the exposure. In fact he appeared
to relish in it, smiling,
his head held high, and waving proudly
at his neighbors
who were calling out to him.

Doug Draime

Unleash the Savage

Unleash the savage
that dwells
in the depths
of your dungeons
with me.

Chris Smith

Dateline

i bring the 6-pack of beer
u make fresh lemonade
and brownies
i bring u flowers... maybe
and condoms, k-y, no rope
i'm here real soon, it's three hours by truck
but i will walk 500 miles for u
i bring beer, magazines and Rolaids, no rope
yeah i'm nervous but excited too
u dry yr hair
or do yr laundry
behind a door
i sit down and wait for u
i a man walk right in and stand or sit
and wait for u
or come towards the door to see u
oh, who r u?
no, who r u? how old r u? just sit right there
i just want to talk, ya know, mentor
that's why i came, ya know, to talk
i'm not doing anything wrong am i?

John J. Trause

Unearthing Stones

unearthing stones
from the moss—
my choked passage
to a place
that never was

Sondra J. Byrnes

It Keeps Coming Back Even Though It Already Came Back

She is a pervasive ghost,
always the tall, the green,
or the brown, the wavy grass,

but here I go, back to Bach again,
leaning /
thinking,
I know how to take care of myself.

Ha! Chop those pills by half!
Genius! You dark, stupid,
germ-infested
snake.

At least, at my lowest, I know
when things are dark,
when death looks enchanting,
I am in the bad ass real world.

I need hospitals at every rest stop.

Lock and chains and feed me with
shovels.

Deep d-minor keeps my arms at
my side,
keeps me from
destroying all that is bad in
my world, all of me.

Carl Heppenstall

A Little Worn

a little worn
but still
serviceable
my mother's heart
was a handmedown.

M. Kei

There Are Days and Days

today is a holiday, tomorrow too, but I forgot which
for I miss you too much to bother with such details
another day stretching that already abysmal void
how can a void get even wider?
it doesn't sound logical but that's what I feel
I had to run away from my apartment
for a couple of hours, lest I lost my mind
the weather was pleasant, so I walked to Place des Ternes
you remember, that pretty square where they sell flowers
then I stopped at the Fnac, the department store which
once harbored the Magasins Réunis
with its lovely art déco façade
how many times did we cover this area together,
going to Parc Monceau, that English-styled
garden Marcel Proust used to mention
in his *Recherche du Temps Perdu*
He too used to live in this neighborhood,
along with Alfred Dreyfus whom Emile Zola
so powerfully defended against the anti-Semites
in his famous *J'accuse.*
Actually there's a plaque nearby mentioning
the French captain whose honor was sullied
for he had resided in the very street where I live
As you know anti-Semitism is again rife in France
as it is all over Europe and in every Muslim country
We all thought that after the Holocaust, the Shoah,
we would never again hear these horrendous words:
Dirty Jews, death to the Heebs and now, death to Israel
thank God (is there really a God?) the Chinese people,
the Indians, mainly the Hindus, most of black Africa,
at least the Christian and animistic folk,
who have suffered from both
European and Arab slavery
and much of America
support us, so we are not alone in this
world where the terrorists want to kill and maim
all those whom they call 'Infidels'
Sorry, Mamica, this isn't a subject I should raise with you

but whenever I open the radio or switch on the TV
all we hear and see are massacres, mainly perpetrated
by Muslims against other poor Muslims
whether it is in Africa, the Middle East or Pakistan
What savagery! Instead of building and progressing,
all those retarded fundamentalists think of
is death and destruction, more death and more destruction
Basta, you're right Mamica, enough with this
have a good evening and bless us all.

Albert Russo

Afternoon Love Tanka

these
afternoon love tanka
between myself
and a nameless soul
i hide even from the wind.

Matsukaze

Hours Are Drifting

Hours are drifting
in and out of knowing.
Outside it begins again.
Stones sleep
close together
in a morning rain.

Ylva Knutsson

Headliners

Maples have sprung their spring buds.
Crows harry the red-tailed raptor,
every damn thing is bold.
In the season of bird-clangor
and territory claimants, headlines squabble,
tea parties break up, March Hare smashes
April's sugar bowl, census takers
swarm the ghettos, everyone knows
unemployment's under-reported.

Rabbits have birthed spring kits,
brown bats die, in droves, of white-nose virus,
gray squirrels suckle their young
in leafy dreys in city trees.
On the breeze, the earliest pollen.
On the earth, white litter of bloodroot petals
and paper cup lids, robin scratching out
its grubs. What is bold is foolhardy
and obvious. Nothing's fair. Follow
the daily news. Follow the raptor,
its reckless, perfect, useful dive.

Ann Michael

Chili Pepper Lights

chili pepper lights
and potted chili plants
both red this evening

M. Kei

That Damn Scent

that damn scent!
crushed magnolias
and vanilla
her exasperation darker
than her plum gown.

Matsukaze

Here and Gone

Crayola Crayon Colors Retired to the Hall of Fame on August 6, 1990

for Stephanie Lynne

Orange-Red	In the beginning the morning sun Was orange red, And orange red I colored it, And now it's gone.
Orange-Yellow	Later on the sun's hot ray Was orange yellow, And orange yellow I colored it Throughout the day.
Lemon Yellow	The noonday sun now over me Was lemon yellow, And lemon yellow I colored it Over land and sea.
Maize	The afternoon, drawn on and on, Was maize like cornfields, And cornfield maize I colored it, And now it's gone.
Green-Blue	Late afternoon the sky, grown dark, Was now green blue, And deep green blue I colored it Beyond the park.
Violet-Blue	When evening came, the nighttime sky Was violet blue, And violet blue I colored it, Gone by and by.

Blue Gray	A giant cloud, drawn over me,
	Was dark blue gray,
	And dark blue gray I colored it,
	Too dark to see.

Raw Umber	My dreams of slumber round my head
	Were deep raw umber,
	And deep raw umber I colored them —
	All gone to bed.

Some old friends from my childhood
Are now all gone,
And here are new ones, one for each,
And all are good

Vivid Tangerine	Jungle Green	Teal Blue	Dandelion
Cerulean	Fuchsia	Royal Purple	Wild Strawberry

John J. Trause

The Mourning

she drops the roses
on the fresh earth;
it is too early
in the mourning

Michael Seese

Leave My Mask

Leave my mask
till sorrow fades
my eyes say
everything
you need to know

anonymous

Falling into the Flower

A flower touches almost everyone's heart.

—Georgia OKeeffe, from her Red Poppy, 1927

The woman fell into the flower, the heart
of the flower. First, it was easy, she fell
deep into black, the poppy center flamed
scarlet around her. Satin petals
caressed her limbs like symphonies as she slid
past dark to a violet surprise.

She had never fallen into living
flowers, their efforts to stay
so poignant she couldn't bear their dying
or her own brief joy. This was a secret she told
no one, just as her descents into painted
flowers were a passion so private they
seemed forbidden.

Her journey into the trumpet flower,
white and shadows of white like whispers.
Was it not shameful to disappear, curving
down into silence? Or the lure of the riotous
green, tangerine, chartreuse and those unbearable
flecks of fire inside the dance of yellow
petals—sunflower O'Keefe had painted
for Maggie, who must have known the same
seduction, still life that blooms past death.

Donna Spector

Shallow Grave

My wife's belly like a giant navel orange
Provides the racetrack. The technician
This time, is not a robot. She circles
The pregnant belly to the left, as race

Car drivers do. I tell the human tech
The Doctor has already buried our fetus
In a shallow grave. The bell racetrack has

dried and the tech shakes the tube and spooges
more purple-pink goo. I watch the belly-button
quiver. The gooey gunk looks like candy
working itself loose on a taffy puller. Slow

heartbeat my wife says. The tech adjusts the screen
and nudges a few buttons. The heartbeat is like
a grade school band: nervous, ducking, unsure.

The song is older than birdsong and slow. My fifteen
year old's, she says, was slower than this. The human
tech smiles and regales my wife with stories. What a
pain in the ass that kid is sometimes. Teenagers

she says. I'm thinking how much I love that kid.

Richard Lee Zuras

Coming Home

Krakow
my town
where a gaunt dragon swallows coins straight off a child's hand
my home
where a beggar's finger points at my bag
and my memories sail over the roof tops, past the sleeping bells
my haven
where tired ghosts of pigeons past
land on cars, trodden stones and my arms
where, once upon a time, men and women
marched
re-writing history with fists made of clay
my shelter
where, once a girl, I wanted to set the world on fire
then grew up and joined the ranks of the snaky
queue to the International Departures Lounge
today I am back
I bite into a piece of the local bread
a cumin seed
gets stuck between my teeth

Elwira Danak

Openings

What if the truth is so elusive because to speak it
is to destroy it,
to contain it; it lies far off
in space or time -
and to see it is to be consumed by it -
to lose one's name,
like a song that disappears into the wind,
or the dream of a hot dance
in a cool river...
the brief appearance of a meadow flower:
to be the being of the changeable.
I love to see that sad and lonely dance
growing out of the cracks in the earth,
reaching for the limitless sky
and the mysteriously unknowable sunlight.
Is it too plainly spoken?
I do not wish to go alone.

Chris Gropp

I Imagine

I imagine
how your lips move
as you read this;
lazy ocean waves
licking burnt horizon.

Hank Archer

I Leave the Weeds

I leave the weeds
knowing what little time
we both have left...
seven years old
in the thickest weeds
with bugs so loud
you can hardly hear me
hiding

Roary Williams (Coyote Sings)

Summer Paradise

We have been having daunting dreams in winter sunset breeze
We have been chasing clouds, staring at starlight rays and wishing
on the shooting star in midnight darkness
This summer paradise we dream of is like sun shooting down on
our warm bodies
Dashed in sands, sprawled out near the waves of the beach and
nature's finest at its very
best

Perching birds, coconut trees swaying to the tune of breezy air, the
summer breeze rocks
us as a lullaby slowly we sleep
Passing hours, unknown time,
Carefree,
No worries under sun.

Christena Williams

Predator

A hook-tooth protrudes.
A lupine snarl. My dog, rapt
in ancestral dreams.

Marion Adams

Running Down

running down
the ragged edge
of the ocean
chasing starfish
back into the sky

Roary Williams (Coyote Sings)

A Long Winter

This year most everything's
late, even ladyslippers
wearing pink tutus. Trilliums,

white and pale pink,
fade by June's second week.
Gay-

wings, hardly higher
than my big toe,
lavender the forest floor

near pitcher plants,
open-mouthed,
brazen.

Kenneth Pobo

If I Could Be

if I could be
sax
of blue breaths
just for you
i would
be blue as twilight
n whisper bruises
blue between your lips

Beez Laine

A Blue Note

Down a street that isn't Bourbon,
that lies as far from New Orleans
as New Jersey, New York or New Caledonia,
a blue note from a tenor sax
escapes the dive door
- mocks the overfilled suit -
and curls like smoke around the streetlight.
Two lovers exchange a look
as though they know the tune,
or one like it, played on a xylophone
or theremin with a bebop twist.
They pass the suit whose open-mouthed face
is tilted up at where the minim
passed out of sight
- but not out of mind.
In the club,
the only thing missing
is the smoke.
Inside there are more blue notes
than people.

Ewan Lawrie

Sabbath Morning

Sabbath morning
going down to the sea
and raising the sail
a white prayer
going up to the sky

M. Kei

Ah

water

   lily
    blossom
       white
         guitar
           playing
             nobody

strumming

Kenneth Pobo

Kinship Chiaroscuro

Now is the season of named storms:
    the noon light leaves rich shadows
    where the trees keep their secrets,
    and all waters are swollen.
The panther is fire despite his silver
    now blue under clouds;
    perfect as consort,
    he nuzzles my humid curls and
    places his eye to mine; so sweet even
    redwoman accepts his gentle teeth
    aloof amid oceans of wheat.
She never forgets her stolen children,
    yet allows her lips to quiver in pleasure;
    hers are the kisses light and brief.
We hear the panther breathing
    all our shoulders touch
    as we curve into each other
    in silence, in silence
    ours is thus our language so

Su Zi

The Chill Breath of Autumn

Chill breath of autumn
clutching at my skin - tonight
bears mortality
within its darkness, cold air
laced with urgency.

Kagen Aurencz Zethmayr

Step Father

He forgets that he used to call me *mariconcito*
that I harbored years of hatred toward him
while hoping to find my real father. My
childhood memories of him reminding me
I was my mother's son, not his. I tried
to poison him once and scattered sharp nails
inside the shoes in his closet. By the time one
of his sons died of AIDS I was already lost
in contempt for the man I blamed for everything.
There was the time I was in love and he met my
boyfriend. Now he forgets to go to the bathroom

or where he is but he still remembers Michael
and asks about him. I help him walk slowly
outdoors to step outside the prison cell that is
the tiny apartment with no windows in which
I grew up abused by both of them. He barely
understands. His fate has been torture. I know
that I cannot be his savior. I used to pray for
him to die but here he is slowly fading. In his
eyes I see that he learned to love me and wishes
he could take it all back. He is unable to recall
those drunken nights and hateful words. I should

do the same. I left a long time ago but he still
remains haunted by the little boy who wanted
to belong. Like him, I want to forget that we
made mistakes and caused so much pain. I need
for both of us to remember how he taught me
how to ride a bike and how to swim and told
me, better late than never, that he loved me and
was proud of all I had done. I have to help him
settle into his favorite chair and let him know that
I forgive him. There is a place somewhere where
he will call me hijo and I will know him as my dad.

Emanuel Xavier

Her Father's Voice

her father's voice
sharp
like thorns of a wilted rose
drunk beneath the sun

Beez Laine

Remembering

Remembering
her mama say,
Close your eyes, baby
and that highway sounds
like a River

W.O.

Acid Rain

The sun has not yet risen.
Rainwater invades the cracks in my window frames,
the windows shake against the wind.

I try to cover the cracks with my bare hands
and fail, leaving water to pour in unattended.
The silence after thunder is quieter than death.

Every autumn you appear in a dream,
Yom Kippur — my birthday, usually.
A day to atone for sins and unsorted memories.

Hail batters my window, summer ice
cast down from a sky devoid of light:
the seasons forgot to change.

Father, for nearly 20 years I have kept your letters,
storing them in a yellow bag that I crammed
in a box to block out all the light.

I am still afraid of the dark,
even if it stops decay;
my hands are stained

with streaks of saltwater,
flesh threatening to bleed
in the burning of acid rain.

The scent of an evening eight years ago
when all the light drained from your eyes;
a colorless reflection of the empty sky.

Beneath my window, the river moves with the rain.
I wonder if the river ever felt invaded
or anything at all.

Tiara Winter-Schorr

I Go in Secret

I go in secret
somber silence
pay the toll
an open heart.

Chris Smith

Old Maple

old maple —
one third left
bent and misshapen
breathless
in the autumn dawn

M. Kei

Name Dropping for a Deceased Wife

for Beth Partlow-Draime

I never thought I'd look back on
her in memory. She seemed so
fastened to her being and her
extraordinary perception
of the world! I watched her joy when she
read Joyce and Kafka,
Chandler and Hammet, or James Cain …
and even William Morris
and Lovecraft. And the times she appeared
to be mesmerized by
Erik Satie and Brahms, Van Morrison,
and Leonard Cohen,
playing on our
boom box
as she tended
the tomatoes
and squash in
the garden behind our house in Echo Park.
And the many passionate and lazy afternoons,
her red hair entwined
through my fingers as I
held up each strand to
the sunlight
steaming through our
bedroom windows.

There were her cryptic
post cards from
across the U.S.
on the way home to see her folks
in Kokomo. The one from
a bus station somewhere
in Texas said simply,
"I'm just listening."

There is no getting away
from her courageous and
passionate struggle
to get the oppressed
Soviet Jews out
of Russia; and there is a tree planted
for her
in Israel.
She made the *bigtime*
when her friend,
Si, published an article
about her in
the L.A. Times
Boris Penson and Mikhail Baryshnikov are in her debt.
But mostly I remember the way she held a
drinking glass full of *Jameson's* whiskey
like it was a China tea cup.
Every moment of those
three years
are somewhere in
my memory
like soft gray rain
falling
inside
a perfect
white cloud.

Doug Draime

A Green Valley

a green valley
but my mother bleeding
red, red, so red
these are the secret things
a child never forgets

M. Kei

Scars

Lying in bed after the first time,
we map each other,
first the footpaths of my freckles

headed for the heart
past the frozen pond
burned by a probe

hot from the belly of a jet.
It touched and took
away the thinnest crepe of flesh.

Across both wrists, a picket
fence of stitches,
the razor cuts of first love.

Now you.

Nothing?
No cuts of baby-falling chin or cheek?

Not even the purple faultlines
or valley rifts of surgery?
Whole, are you? Untouched?

Everything in and on you
that you started with, nothing you didn't?

But wait—what's that

you're trying to hide,
that quarter moon
inside your thigh,

from the tin can
of the rooftop rescue
of a kitten

when you fell?

That's what I want

to be—the one you save.

The one that leaves a scar.

William Greenway

After a Lie

after a lie -
the sound of my heart
and a leaf, falling

Sandi Pray

Unshatter

as much as i try
i cannot unshatter
the glass of my life

Michael Seese

What Am I

what am I
but a memory
of myself
surrounded
by memories of others

Alyona Schatzman

Most Times

most times, Abba
i am afraid of death
i often pause
during random days
looking toward You for comfort.

Matsukaze

Depression Lifting

A misty veil drowns the oars
that break the stillness
of morning.
The brightness
of guessed at sunlight
catches ripples
as shadows pass.
A heron silhouetted
against bright water,
cast in bronze,
is still.
As day alights
and I awake
parting the curtains of sleep
I step from dream
to dream.

Paul Smith

Three Quarters Dead

Wistful stars
in the evening
a little white
with memory and
a handful of dust

Gary Tynam

The Year's Best

the year's best
bad day—the car
broken down
on a sunny Sunday
and a hitchhike home

M. Kei

Beyond the Trees

Beyond the trees
A river within his soul
Floating paper boats

Rhonda Brockmeyer

I Sing of Viking Ships and Rivers

*On the deaths of Ingmar Bergman and Michelangelo Antonioni
on July 30, 2007*

Från sperm till spöke : Al di là delle nuvole

*Hinter dem Nicht-sehen-wollen, hinter seiner Leugnung des Lebens
steht immer das Wissen, dass das Leben, dass die Welt der Dinge
stärker ist als er. Es ist, als wollte ein Sklave, der in Träumen ehrgeizing
und herrschsüchtig ist, seinen Herrn und die Knute beseitigen, indem er
sie leugnet. Genau wie [Oscar] Wilde eben durch seinen Spott auf das
Evangelium bewies, dass es vorhanden war, dass es für ihn vorhanden
war. Der wirkliche Heide ignoriert es, weil er auch wirklich kaum von
ihm weiss.*

Felix Paul Greve, Randarabesken zu Oscar Wilde *(1903)*

A Viking ship turned tumulus
lies buried on an isle,
or was it put upon the sea
and set on fire in style?
So set adrift in northern seas
it burns, or stands a pile.
It burns no more and stands for nothing;
it drifts in swill and bile.

        A voyage on the river Po
        in misty nebulosity,
        a steamer tramp or cargo ship,
        a giant red monstrosity
        pulled into port... beyond the clouds,
        a witness to atrocity,
        it drifts through stratocumulus
        in turbid luminosity,
        in secret reciprocity.

Jefferson lives... not.

Styx
Acheron
Cocytus

Phlegethon

Lethe

NOTE: *Från sperm till spöke* (From Sperm to Spook) and *Al di là delle nuvole* (Beyond the Clouds) are the names of two projects by Bergman and Antonioni respectively, the former a play found incomplete among Bergman's papers, and the latter a realized film by Antonioni. The epigraph comes from Paul Morris's translation of Greve: Behind his unwillingness to see, behind his denial of life was the knowledge that life, the world of reality, was stronger than he. It is as if a slave, ambitious and domineering in his dreams, were to eliminate his master and the knout by denying them. Just so, Wilde, precisely through his mockery of it, proved that the gospel was present, that it was present for him. The real pagan ignores the gospel, because he knows little about it.

John J. Trause

The Final Word

Heart drawn at tide's turn
Heart carved on a fallen oak
Love: the final word.

Marion Adams

Elegant Still

R.C. deWinter

A Feature on Bauke Kamstra

We conducted a two-part interview with artist and writer Bauke Kamstra (some may know him by his Twitter handle, @Wyrde). Kamstra's approach to our questions illustrates his grace with words and his unique mentality about life, art, and creative mysticism. Some answers are given as poetry and some are given as prose, but all contain the lyricism of a man who recognizes language as a tool and an instrument. The following conversation is not always linear or traditional but is full of music, poetry, life, and constant reminders that humanity reaches toward art as a means of connecting to a collective divinity.

Let's talk about your background and young life. When did your parents leave Europe? What influence, if any, did that background have on your development?

I was born in Halifax, Nova Scotia, a port city on the far east coast of Canada. Once, before my birth, there was a very large explosion there. Many people were killed. Much of the city was destroyed. Heroes were born in the wreckage. A link and a love was forged with Boston, who brought much rescue. My birth was not nearly this traumatic.

Dutch immigrant parents
fleeing the dark wreckage
that was Europe.

A familiar story.

That port city
drowning in sailors
in cargo
let them go into the valley
a land full of apples & tides
& fierce grim men.

I was taken by force
yet to be fair
I was only a baby
their property
& did not know what to decide.

The Annapolis Valley was a common, insular, self-absorbed place with gangs of rough farm boys, mountain boys, town boys, teaching each other the error of ways.

Longfellow wrote the poem "Evangeline" about the tragic expulsion of the Acadians (from nearby Grand Pre, in the valley), when France lost to Britain and deeded the colony to them.

At 15, in the full rigor of my teenage years I fled this history, the apples and tides, the rowdy boys of whom so many died, wrecked in cars and beer fumes. I felt as if forced to leave, as once the Acadians had been expelled into the world.

I had learned to flip a burger
& wash a dish
my hands were just beginning
to make marks
that looked like things.

I joined the diaspora of hitchhikers that were already lined up at exits from coast to coast, waiting for a ride.

The roads were not lonely
they were an open
constant traffic of souls
cars, hearts, minds
another golden age.

We came down from the hills
& up from the plains
looking to wet our feet
in different seas.

We knew that those
come before us
were mistaken
so we set out to make
a better world.

As they did.

You've lived an itinerant lifestyle in the past. How has travel affected your spirituality and your approach to poetry?

Those were halcyon years, fishing like kings. As I traveled coast to coast, across Canada, the U.S., forays far south into Mexico. Working cafes, restaurants, carnival rides, whatever it took to make a few bucks and keep moving. I learned to play a bamboo flute, to call spirits from rocks, and many other obscure and esoteric things (I scarcely knew half of what I did). I made mistakes, a habit I haven't give up. I made a few better marks, slowly improved my image skills.

Always I asked questions. Only rarely was there anyone else there. I had experiences that were strange, mystical, inexplicable, even to myself. (E.g.: Unearthly singing late at night, camped in a field of yarrow, nothing around for miles.)

I'd been brought up a holy roller. In Vegas I had a lucky streak and became a high roller. So I fled (I was always fleeing) to the Middle East, India, up to Nepal. I'd had a little grounding in university philosophy by then, though it didn't take, and I tried to learn something by treading holy ground. No matter where I looked, I didn't see God.

There is no reason
a finger
an eye
or a thought
can be laid on god.

Every act
is mystical
every poem
a mysticism.

The answer
to the question of god
is possibility.

The holy books

are possibilities
the tarot
is possibility
the interpretation
of the alignment
of stars
is possibility
runes
hieroglyphs
alchemy
the kabbalah
reincarnation
heaven & hell
Taoism
the I Ching
(especially)
are possibilities.

Poems
images
are possibilities.

The laundry
& the dishes
are also
possibilities.

The question is not the answer.

Without answers, I eventually came to rest. To find focus I intensified my preoccupation with beauty. I spent a year in art school, developing craft. I also worked there as a model, flipping from one side of the canvas to the other, like a spinning coin.

What life events, if any, spurred the transition from artist to a poet?

I discovered nakedness. The wearing of clothes, I learned, is a symbolic act. The strange, North American puritan ethic is strongly rooted in this, civilization is also invested in it. Protection from the elements is an occasionally useful side effect. One of the primary purposes seems to be to tacitly ignore the physical, the animal. This does not necessarily work. Some use it to accentuate. The hidden is more alluring than the exposed.

As the clothes fall away
a butterfly from the cocoon
complete
and resplendent

in the absence
of layers
of deceit.

Clothing is no more than a mask. Its layers conceal, and we learn to hide within them. I found that the removal of clothing not only revealed the beauty of the body, but that the unveiling exposed layers of the heart, the mind, the soul. The one exposure led to other exposures, in a cascading process of permission and freedom.

I drew and painted mostly women. This was not so much an impulse of heterosexuality. I was not blind to the beauty of men. Women seemed more comfortable with nakedness, more in love, or more obsessed, with their own bodies. They were more curious about how it looked in the eyes of others. Women are mysterious, men transparent. I suppose this may be true of both genders, that their own is deducible, while the other isn't, I don't know. What I know is that this mystery enhances beauty beyond normal bounds, to the edge of divinity.

A tiny Picasso girl
with half grapefruit breasts
long nose
eyebrow wings

a tiny serious mouth
that knows
how to smile.

In every drawing, in every painting, I attempted to reveal the unveiling, the nakedness beyond the body, and the allure of the mystery.

Art and poetry have strong similarities for me. Both are a search for meaning, for beauty. I enter an unordinary space, with different rules. Everything I know is there with me, as well as everything I don't. Only a little memory follows me when I come out of that space, but it doesn't matter, because I have the image, or the poem. Generally, the deeper in I go, the more profound the work that comes out. This is the experience I think of meditation: ecstatic, non-thinking, a simultaneous sinking deeper into the world, and an expansion into the void. This experience is somewhat describable within an image, or in poetry, poorly with logic or reason.

Which poets have had the most influence on you in the last year or so? At any time?

Influence is pervasive, it is in all things. Who in western culture, for example, has not seen the Mona Lisa. Influence is not reducible to structured form. For every influence one can name, there are another hundred influences lurking below consciousness. My family, my childhood, my travelling, my art, all are major influences on my work. Yet to name any particular incident is both true and false. No such statement can be made without leaving something crucial out, most likely something that has not yet risen (or never will rise) to consciousness.

The ideas of "favorites" or "best" are born in competition, which requires a winner, an elite. To me, the best flavor of ice cream is the one in my mouth. Every poem is transcendental, if only in some small way. I constantly seek that element of mini-satori, a zen-koanish stopping of the world, so that the reader (and I) gain a different perception of the world forever, even if infinitesimally small. Such soups become large mixed with others in the pot of time.

Today I am reading Leonard Cohen. Today he is my greatest influence. Tomorrow I will read Don Coles or Jeni Couzyn, or perhaps I will read Patrick Lane, or Jonathan Aaron, and they will be my greatest influences. Or an anthology. I read voraciously every day.

The history of art is not only the sacred / psychic / psychological / sociological but the physical / technological as well. What are the alternatives to paint & brush? When might art have taken an entirely different route, a series of possibilities never played out?

In the forest
root twines with root
branches rub
leaves breathe the same air
supporting the wings
of birds.

Branches
moss
earth
are pathways
trails for
insects & animals.

All one
made of many.

The influence of ideas spreads like a virus. For example, the idea of evolution was created and we began to think of many things in those terms, as ascending (or descending) processes. Steam power, electricity, computers, and we begin see things in mechanistic terms, intelligence as programming, as software. There are many examples of this, from psychology to physics. We are all invaded by our social / psychological milieu. All of this is reflected in language, and is inescapable, except, perhaps, by poetry.

I've fought against these things, struggled to escape them, persistently, futilely. I perceived the obvious falseness of language, its inability to be precise, to be true. I thought words were lies and abandoned them for image. Even so, my artwork was gestural, depending as much on accident as intent and control. My most powerful pieces did not rely so much on an abundance of sensuality as by the prominence of ambiguity.

How would you define poetry?

Poetry is the eye of language.

Language is paradox
only poetry can breathe.

It is not language
but the silence in language
that needs poetry to be heard.

Poetry arrived for me at a convergence: the realization that it embodied the same communicative power of ambiguity that image does was one, and the desperation for another form of expression was another, as arthritis made making visual art increasingly difficult.

My arthritis
is a wandering drunk
visiting a
different joint
every night.

What kind of milieu do you prefer when you write? How do you structure and approach your writing life?

I write every day. I write by hand. I normally go out and find a place brimming with solitude, and most often before the sun rises.

When I write the initial poem, the impetus is spirit and heart, and a touch of mind. I enter a kind of meditative state and the poems come out. Sometimes the poem is already done. More often I apply mind, revising the poems as I transcribe them to my computer. Some poems get revised and revised.

Old hands
old fingers
manipulating pen
or brush.

Trying to explain
a life.

I now read poetry voraciously, omnivorously, as I have read so many things throughout my life. I allow its sediment to filter down deep into mind. This sometimes sets off an inspired train of thought, resulting in a poem. My poems, in some sense, contain the history of poetry. This may be true of all poetry, influence is pervasive.

I have found different ways to acquire craft. A systematic approach is solid, usually faster, but risks rigidity. When I was learning to draw, I thought, I have to made 10,000 bad lines in order to learn to make good lines, so let me get them over with. I apply the same reasoning with poetry.

My involvement with poetics is on a visceral level, not the theoretical. Any theories I may possess about poetics, conscious or otherwise, are embodied in the poems themselves. It is not that I do not think about poetics, I do, constantly. Yet I rely on my gut. I see, for example, complex, intricate, word constructions and I think, wow, this is great, I should do this. Then I don't, for a sparser, simpler line often seems to contain more truth. Then I suddenly find myself writing dense, intricate work. It is not a science, it is an evolution (to use that viral idea). Everything is subject to change.

Committing to a specific style can be an ossification of process. I hope to avoid this, to continue to expand and learn new ways of writing, of poetry.

I do have preferences of environment that make writing easier for me. Before I started writing poetry I wrote an (unpublished) book on overcoming creative blocks. I am not blocked (I was once subject to them). I am currently working on a project to turn this book into a course on creativity (engagement, inspiration, production, & breaking blocks).

Anything from the mundane to the esoteric is a fit subject for poetry. I generate my own prompts as easily as waking up.

When you think

this is no day for poetry
it is the perfect day for poetry.

Could you tell us more about what went into your book, *Reaching Out?* **What prompted you to write a book at this stage in your life, what did you learn in the process, etc.**

My book, *Reaching Out*, was premature and the issue was craft. Craft without inspiration is mostly decoration. Inspiration without craft sometimes succeeds, but more often fails. I had made a few thousand micropoems, and a hundred or so longer poems. It wasn't enough. I have now written in excess of 10,000 micropoems and several hundred longer poems and I now intend to come out with a new book, most likely by the time this interview is printed.

The book will be called: *Flower & River; Bone & Stone*. The hermetically complex ideas associated with the elements emerge in many forms, and I use these elements to section the book (or chapbook, I'm not sure what it should be called). Even so, I do not attempt to force the poetry, the esoteric implications, on the book. The poems arise naturally out of the elements I have chosen. There are deep connections within that which is most common and mundane.

I plan to pre-sell a limited number of signed copies that will be accompanied by personalized poems, written for the purchaser, and inscribed by hand onto a greeting card that has one of my images on it.

I will be putting this on my blog at www.positivelywyrde.com

Why do crows resonate with you in much of your work?

Crows are the messenger
They are the bringers of the word
They bring fire
write omens on air
arrive before the battle
are intimate with death
clean up after
fly direct, unswerving
speak with voices harsh
   with the sound of truth

They are sacred, mystical, magical
cross worlds

They are raucous
& they are rude
wary, but unafraid
& love shiny objects.

They steal eggs, but will fight
   an eagle to protect the nest
often alone they
   congregate at night.

They are black, as night is black
   & hide in it.
& obvious by day
And when summer birds go
   they stay.

What advice do you have for young poets?

I am a young poet. Only the body is ageing. I will say this:

We do not entirely have to be, yet are normally limited by the preconceptions of our culture, by the virus of ideas that infect us, by the assumptions of our parents and our peers. Poetry, art, is about boundaries, and about crossing boundaries. An artwork is necessarily limited by its frame, a poem by language and form.

Even so, successful art is always bigger than its bounds, conceptually, spiritually, and / or in other ways, striking deep, striking wide, & flying high. The limitations are as illusory as the world itself. This is what the artist discovers.

The process is as simple and complex as learning to see, instead of look. To notice the spaces between, instead of just objects, notice that there are no edges - there are, at most, corners. Notice that everything is connected and that there is always a mystery.

Without sun
I would not know
the beauty
of your nakedness

without the moon
I would not know
its mystery.

I am immersed in sensuality. Beauty seizes me and shakes my soul, leaves me breathless, and sometimes weeping for joy. Input comes from the world, through our senses, including those extra ones that perceive beyond the physical. These are subtle enough that we are never quite sure of them. They are not concrete, that work on the edges of things, as much in the realm of possibility as actuality. Input is accepted holistically. It is a misunderstanding to think soul, heart, mind & body are separate. They are integrated.

In previous interviews, you've described writing poetry as a form of meditation that allows you to enter a certain mental space where the conscious mind brings back material that the unconscious mind has collected. Could you talk more about that mental space and what poetry as a spiritual act has to offer?

There is little I truly know. I have many, many ideas about things, and even a few unsupportable beliefs. (Warning, these are subject to change without notice.)

Ego is a tiny veneer of thought and personality that believes it is you.

My mind thinks it is me.

Consciousness is vast, the subconscious is vaster by orders of magnitude. Contained within the subconscious, & containing it, is a connectivity to everything, by spirit, by physics, by processes we have little or no conception of.

Language is mnemonic, a system of pointing signs, not communication. I believe all real communication takes place on an empathic level. Thus, for example, in reading a book, or viewing artwork, or talking face to face, we use the symbols embedded in these languages to take us emphatically to its meaning, directly from the author, whether in front of you, separated by space, or separated by a thousand years of time. Miscommunication takes place when you confuse language with meaning, or allow your preconceptions to rule.

All of this information is encoded in what Jung might call the collective unconscious, or something else. I think it is much bigger than that, access to an accumulation of infinite information. The medium that embodies this could be a substrate of life, of reality, or something unknown. This information is available to the individual subconscious, and will sometimes surface consciously.

The physical world is an illusion. Time & space are illusions. Life & death are illusions. Convincing illusions.

No energy is ever lost. We are most likely infinite & eternal. Ego is an ephemeral phenomena associated with being corporate.

I look forward to finding out more.

Art asks questions
in a language of light
I write
in the language of sight.

Contributor Biographies

Hank Archer is a journalist who has only recently begun writing poetry. He takes inspiration from every aspect of the human experience. He plays in a rockabilly band, drinks coffee, and lives in Canada.

L.B. Austin was once a poet without a muse, then once upon a time, in the early hours of a spring dawn, his sleep heavy whispers slipped their kisses within her soul, and so the story began. Now she write of love & lust, of the beauty hidden in the trinkets of this old world, of souls meeting on thirsty lips, of wrath and rage, and of hungry fingertips.

Grace Brignolle is originally from Ecuador but has spent most of her life in New York City. She studied Graphic Design and Photography in college but deferred a career in the arts when her first child was born. Her obsession with street photography began years ago, but she also loves photographing the human body and dogs.

Rhonda Brockmeyer is a Canadian poet & artist passionately inspired by the beauty and power of the natural world. You can find her site at rhondalbrockmeyer.wordpress.com.
Follow @VespersAria on Twitter for micro poetry & photography.

Sondra J. Byrnes is relatively new to writing poetry. It started three years ago when she realized that Twitter is a good forum for short form poetry. She writes haiku, senryu, tanka and other micropoetry forms. Her poetry has been published in *Tuck magazine, Prune Juice, World Haiku Review, Ribbons, Notes from the Gean* and other poetry journals; it is also included in the anthology *Fragments* by Blue Flute. Along with short form poetry, Byrnes is interested in ikebana and chanoyu. Byrnes is a retired law and business professor from the University of Notre Dame; she lives in South Bend, Indiana.

Graeme Cooper is a high school English teacher from Scotland. He was a poet for twenty years before writing his first poem and could convince himself that the world was an illusion, if only that damned bird would stop singing.

Ryan Catherine Derham is a 24 year old writer who lives on the east coast of the United States. She spent a year in France after graduating from college, pursuing her dreams. She is currently working on her first novel and a book of poems.

Alec Goldwyn began taking photos at the age of 13, when he received his first camera. He holds a bachelor of arts in Anthropology from Stonybrook, State University of NY and a bachelor of science in Aviation Technology from Metropolitan State University of Denver. His travels have taken him to 15 countries spanning 6 continents and 20 states within the U.S. The photos shown here were taken in northern Kenya and China (including Shanghai and the Hunan Province).

Bauke Kamstra is first generation Dutch Canadian born on the edge of the North American continent. An artist for most of his life, he has been writing poetry since long before he ever put it into words. Twitter: @wyrde, Blog: **www.positivelywyrde.com**

M. Kei is a tall ship sailor and award-winning poet. He is the editor-in-chief of *Take Five : Best Contemporary Tanka*, and the editor of *Atlas Poetica : A Journal of Poetry of Place in Contemporary Tanka*. His second collection of poetry, *Slow Motion : The Log of a Chesapeake Bay Skipjack*, is Recommend Reading by the Chesapeake Bay Project. He also the author of *Fire Dragon*, an Asian-themed fantasy / science fiction novel with a gay hero. He can be followed on Twitter @kujakupoet, or visit AtlasPoetica.org.

Ylva Knutsson was born in 1973 in Sweden and began writing poetry eleven years ago after a life-changing event. Her emotions are the whisper that makes her look for a pen. Selections of her work are forthcoming from a small Swedish publisher. Micropoetry on Twitter is her English debut as a poet.

"Beez" Laine lives in Australia. Beez started using the Internet three years ago to connect with other writers and share her work using Twitter. She currently has two blogs, msbeez.wordpress.com and beezknez.blogspot.com.au, to present her lengthier written works. Beez's style of writing poetry is mainly freeform but she likes to experiment using her pen to write micropoetry and haiku. Although she enjoys all styles of poetry, her personal preference is writing without boundaries. She derives inspiration from life experience and also from composing music on a piano, where she can translate sound into words.

LazyBookworm is a devotee of the written word in all forms. She is an aspiring poet as well as a wife, mother and full-time cat wrangler. A revolutionary at heart, LazyBookworm was credited with giving the Occupy Wall Street movement its momentum. She is also utterly fascinated with the possibility of time travel.

elle M lives on the north shore of Lake Ontario. She is an artist, writes poetry, captures photographs and collects vintage postcards. She grew up in 'big sky country' Alberta, draws inspiration from long walks and wherever the wind carries her.

Matsukaze is a classical/operatic vocalist, thespian, and minister. He began writing haiku seriously around 2005, and tanka around 2006. He was recently re-introduced to tanka in 2013 by M. Kei, editor of *Atlas Poetica, Journey of Poetry of Place in Contemporary Tanka*. He lives in Louisiana; dividing his time between there and Houston, TX.

W.O. is the mother to three joyful children and works with families experiencing homelessness. She writes to maintain her sanity.

Sandi Pray is a retired high school media specialist living closely with nature in the wilds of the North Carolina mountains and forest marshes of North Florida. Living a vegan lifestyle, she is an avid hiker and lover of all critters.

Alyona Schatzman was born in the former Soviet Union republic of Kazakhstan and now live in Cedarburg, WI. She is fluent in Russian and English. She also enjoys literature, art, classical music, opera, theater, travel, international culture, and philosophy. She started writing poetry in English shortly after joining Twitter and discovering the wonderful world of micropoetry.

Chris Smith is a writer, artist, and entrepreneur who lives with one goal, to express herself and grow. She's a photographer working on her fourth 365 Project, and in January 2013 completed a Project following her Mom through Stage 3 Cancer. Chris writes in a variety of genres, from nonfiction to erotica, and is hammering out three books, and pondering a padded dish room.

Akiko Taylor is a professional translator who was born and brought up in Tokyo, Japan. She currently lives with her two daughters in County Armagh, Northern Ireland. Her poetry writing started in her late 20s, and she enjoys using haiku and tanka forms the best. She is a humanist and does not like creating boundaries or being enclosed by them.

Roary Williams / Coyote Sings is a micropoet on Twitter (@CoyoteSings). Most people have taken to calling him Coyote, but he is originally from the Detroit area in Michigan. When he first moved to New Mexico in 1989, he was enamored of the land and the skies of the high desert. The desert has taken a part of his soul and given him a chance to see and appreciate life in a whole new way.

Tiara Winter-Schorr is the associate editor at *Poetry Nook* magazine and an emeritus contributor at *Numero Cinq* magazine. A life-long resident of New York City, she graduated from Columbia University with a B.A. in Creative Writing and has a passion for black-and-white photography. She loves all kinds of poetry, personal essays, and fiction. She is currently at work on a novel.

Kagen Aurencz Zethmayr is a freelance artistic / intellectual factotum currently existing in the Chicago suburbs along with a massive accumulation of creative and critical works in various media, sizes and stages of progress. A 1999 graduate of Columbia College Chicago (Self-Designed / Interdisciplinary Arts major), he has been writing and developing his own voice and style in multiple forms for over three fitful decades, but regards poetry as the most directly-efficacious form of "the Muse kicking me in the ass."

Poetry Announcements

Brancusi's Egg

Sara Baker's collection of poems, *Brancusi's Egg*, limns the ordinary passages of a woman's life—the passing of a beloved parent, the parenting of growing children, partnering—as well as the extraordinary experience of living with chronic illness.

Poet Coleman Barks calls *Brancusi's Egg* "….An amazing, fading-away, absolutely unique dance. Very beautiful."

Sara Baker is a novelist, short story writer and poet. Her stories have been published in or are forthcoming in *The Examined Life, The Chattahoochee Review, The New Quarterly, The Spirit that Moves Us, The Habersham Review, The Lullwater Review* and other publications. Her poetry has appeared in *The 2011 Hippocrates Prize for Poetry and Medicine, The Healing Muse, Ars Medica, The Yale Journal of Humanities in Medicine, The Journal of Poetry Therapy,* and elsewhere. She blogs about writing and healing at Word Medicine, www.saratbaker.wordpress.com.

Finishing Line Press
PO Box 1626
Georgetown, KY 40324
859-514-8966
https://finishinglinepress.com

Tamed by the Desert

Diana Woodcock's fourth chapbook, *Tamed by the Desert*, is available for pre-order now from Finishing Line Press. Poet Rachel Hadas, author of *The Golden Road, Relations,* and *The Ache of Appetite,* writes about it: "Diana Woodcock's poetry takes us out into the desert and instructs us in its flora and fauna. But these rich and distinctive poems do more; they invite us into a well-stocked and meditative mind that is not afraid to ponder infinity. In Woodcock's world, Meister Eckhart, Ethiopian hedgehogs, and broad-faced Sand cats are all neighbors under the same enormous sky."

For more information, please visit:

https://finishinglinepress.com/

Nefarious by Emanuel Xavier Coming Out 10/15 from Rebel Satori Press

Emanuel Xavier is an acclaimed writer—often referred to as one of the first openly gay Nuyorican poets and founder of contemporary mariposa lit. With heartfelt honesty and humor, _Nefarious_ is a poetry collection that welcomes the reader into the second act of a former underage prostitute.

Nefarious captures insights into his private world; relationships, heartbreaks, life as a spoken word artist, time spent with his cat, aging. With a dose of dark humor, Xavier's pleasure in the written word and his passion makes this an engaging collection.

The Rites of Stone

The two most recent poetry books published by Robert Lima are *The Rites of Stone* (2010; ISBN 978-0-940804-02-9) and *SEL:F* (2012; ISBN 978-0-940804-03-6) both published by The Orlando Press and available at Amazon.com and BN.com.

Edge of the Pond

Edge Of The Pond, Selected haiku and tanka, by Darrell Lindsey, was published by Popcorn Press (2012). It contains many of his Japanese short form poems that have won international awards. It is also available on Amazon (including Kindle), amazon.co.uk, tower.com, and BN.com. Lindsey's work is also included in *Haiku In English: The First Hundred Years* (W.W. Norton, 2013), which features an introduction by Billy Collins, former United States Poet Laureate.

Life Work

Poetry and life are interwoven in Charlotte Mandel's latest book titled *Life Work*, published by David Robert Books. The poems explore the progress of a loving marriage into loss and transcendence, as well as homage to artists and concern for the effects of war on humanity and nature. The collection creates a tapestry of classic and original forms with rich imagery and precision. Information and sample poems at:

http://www.davidrobertbooks.com/mandel.html.

Visit the author at www.charlottemandel.com

Credits

"a green valley" first appeared in *Atlas Poetic: A Journal of Poetry of Place* #1, Spring 2008, as part of a tanka sequence, "Bridal Veil Falls."

"Dante and We" first appeared in *Living in the Nature Poem*, by Mary Harwell Sayler.

"Insomnia Cantatas" first appeared in *The Ledge* #29, 2005.

"Monsoon Lessons" first appeared in *The Christian Science Monitor* in 1977.

"Sabbath morning" was an Honorable Mention San Francisco Haiku Poets Tanka Contest, 2008, and first appeared in print in *Mariposa* 20.

"Summer Paradise" first appeared in *Inner Child Magazine*.

www.ingramcontent.com/pod-product-compliance
Lightning Source LLC
Chambersburg PA
CBHW021127020426
42331CB00005B/658